Mom's Handy
LITTLE BUSY BEE
Daily Life Planner

I0691147

ACTIVINOTES

Activinotes

DAILY JOURNALS, PLANNERS, NOTEBOOKS AND OTHER BLANK BOOKS

Expenses

Agenda

To do list

MONDAY	TUESDAY	WEDNESDAY
BREAKFAST:	BREAKFAST:	BREAKFAST:
LUNCH:	LUNCH:	LUNCH:
DINNER:	DINNER:	DINNER:
SNACKS:	SNACKS:	SNACKS:

THURSDAY	FRIDAY	SATURDAY	SUNDAY
BREAKFAST:	BREAKFAST:	BREAKFAST:	BREAKFAST:
LUNCH:	LUNCH:	LUNCH:	LUNCH:
DINNER:	DINNER:	DINNER:	DINNER:
SNACKS:	SNACKS:	SNACKS:	SNACKS:

NOTES:

Expenses

Agenda

To do list

MONDAY	TUESDAY	WEDNESDAY
BREAKFAST:	BREAKFAST:	BREAKFAST:
LUNCH:	LUNCH:	LUNCH:
DINNER:	DINNER:	DINNER:
SNACKS:	SNACKS:	SNACKS:

THURSDAY	FRIDAY	SATURDAY	SUNDAY
BREAKFAST:	BREAKFAST:	BREAKFAST:	BREAKFAST:
LUNCH:	LUNCH:	LUNCH:	LUNCH:
DINNER:	DINNER:	DINNER:	DINNER:
SNACKS:	SNACKS:	SNACKS:	SNACKS:

NOTES:

_____
_____
_____
_____
_____
_____
_____
_____
_____
_____
_____
_____
_____
_____
_____
_____
_____
_____
_____
_____
_____
_____

Expenses

Agenda

To do list

MONDAY	TUESDAY	WEDNESDAY
BREAKFAST:	BREAKFAST:	BREAKFAST:
LUNCH:	LUNCH:	LUNCH:
DINNER:	DINNER:	DINNER:
SNACKS:	SNACKS:	SNACKS:

THURSDAY	FRIDAY	SATURDAY	SUNDAY
BREAKFAST:	BREAKFAST:	BREAKFAST:	BREAKFAST:
LUNCH:	LUNCH:	LUNCH:	LUNCH:
DINNER:	DINNER:	DINNER:	DINNER:
SNACKS:	SNACKS:	SNACKS:	SNACKS:

NOTES:

Expenses

Agenda

To do list

MONDAY	TUESDAY	WEDNESDAY
BREAKFAST:	BREAKFAST:	BREAKFAST:
LUNCH:	LUNCH:	LUNCH:
DINNER:	DINNER:	DINNER:
SNACKS:	SNACKS:	SNACKS:

THURSDAY	FRIDAY	SATURDAY	SUNDAY
BREAKFAST:	BREAKFAST:	BREAKFAST:	BREAKFAST:
LUNCH:	LUNCH:	LUNCH:	LUNCH:
DINNER:	DINNER:	DINNER:	DINNER:
SNACKS:	SNACKS:	SNACKS:	SNACKS:

NOTES:

_____
_____
_____
_____
_____
_____
_____
_____
_____
_____
_____
_____
_____
_____
_____
_____
_____
_____
_____
_____
_____
_____

Expenses

Agenda

To do list

MONDAY	TUESDAY	WEDNESDAY
BREAKFAST:	BREAKFAST:	BREAKFAST:
LUNCH:	LUNCH:	LUNCH:
DINNER:	DINNER:	DINNER:
SNACKS:	SNACKS:	SNACKS:

THURSDAY	FRIDAY	SATURDAY	SUNDAY
BREAKFAST:	BREAKFAST:	BREAKFAST:	BREAKFAST:
LUNCH:	LUNCH:	LUNCH:	LUNCH:
DINNER:	DINNER:	DINNER:	DINNER:
SNACKS:	SNACKS:	SNACKS:	SNACKS:

NOTES:

Expenses

Agenda

To do list

MONDAY	TUESDAY	WEDNESDAY
BREAKFAST:	BREAKFAST:	BREAKFAST:
LUNCH:	LUNCH:	LUNCH:
DINNER:	DINNER:	DINNER:
SNACKS:	SNACKS:	SNACKS:

THURSDAY	FRIDAY	SATURDAY	SUNDAY
BREAKFAST:	BREAKFAST:	BREAKFAST:	BREAKFAST:
LUNCH:	LUNCH:	LUNCH:	LUNCH:
DINNER:	DINNER:	DINNER:	DINNER:
SNACKS:	SNACKS:	SNACKS:	SNACKS:

NOTES:

_____
_____
_____
_____
_____
_____
_____
_____
_____
_____
_____
_____
_____
_____
_____
_____
_____
_____
_____
_____
_____
_____
_____

Expenses

Agenda

To do list

MONDAY	TUESDAY	WEDNESDAY
BREAKFAST:	BREAKFAST:	BREAKFAST:
LUNCH:	LUNCH:	LUNCH:
DINNER:	DINNER:	DINNER:
SNACKS:	SNACKS:	SNACKS:

THURSDAY	FRIDAY	SATURDAY	SUNDAY
BREAKFAST:	BREAKFAST:	BREAKFAST:	BREAKFAST:
LUNCH:	LUNCH:	LUNCH:	LUNCH:
DINNER:	DINNER:	DINNER:	DINNER:
SNACKS:	SNACKS:	SNACKS:	SNACKS:

NOTES:

Expenses

Agenda

To do list

MONDAY	TUESDAY	WEDNESDAY
BREAKFAST:	BREAKFAST:	BREAKFAST:
LUNCH:	LUNCH:	LUNCH:
DINNER:	DINNER:	DINNER:
SNACKS:	SNACKS:	SNACKS:

THURSDAY	FRIDAY	SATURDAY	SUNDAY
BREAKFAST:	BREAKFAST:	BREAKFAST:	BREAKFAST:
LUNCH:	LUNCH:	LUNCH:	LUNCH:
DINNER:	DINNER:	DINNER:	DINNER:
SNACKS:	SNACKS:	SNACKS:	SNACKS:

NOTES:

Expenses

Agenda

To do list

MONDAY	TUESDAY	WEDNESDAY
BREAKFAST:	BREAKFAST:	BREAKFAST:
LUNCH:	LUNCH:	LUNCH:
DINNER:	DINNER:	DINNER:
SNACKS:	SNACKS:	SNACKS:

THURSDAY	FRIDAY	SATURDAY	SUNDAY
BREAKFAST:	BREAKFAST:	BREAKFAST:	BREAKFAST:
LUNCH:	LUNCH:	LUNCH:	LUNCH:
DINNER:	DINNER:	DINNER:	DINNER:
SNACKS:	SNACKS:	SNACKS:	SNACKS:

NOTES:

Expenses

Agenda

To do list

MONDAY	TUESDAY	WEDNESDAY
BREAKFAST:	BREAKFAST:	BREAKFAST:
LUNCH:	LUNCH:	LUNCH:
DINNER:	DINNER:	DINNER:
SNACKS:	SNACKS:	SNACKS:

THURSDAY	FRIDAY	SATURDAY	SUNDAY
BREAKFAST:	BREAKFAST:	BREAKFAST:	BREAKFAST:
LUNCH:	LUNCH:	LUNCH:	LUNCH:
DINNER:	DINNER:	DINNER:	DINNER:
SNACKS:	SNACKS:	SNACKS:	SNACKS:

NOTES:

Expenses

Agenda

To do list

MONDAY	TUESDAY	WEDNESDAY
BREAKFAST:	BREAKFAST:	BREAKFAST:
LUNCH:	LUNCH:	LUNCH:
DINNER:	DINNER:	DINNER:
SNACKS:	SNACKS:	SNACKS:

THURSDAY	FRIDAY	SATURDAY	SUNDAY
BREAKFAST:	BREAKFAST:	BREAKFAST:	BREAKFAST:
LUNCH:	LUNCH:	LUNCH:	LUNCH:
DINNER:	DINNER:	DINNER:	DINNER:
SNACKS:	SNACKS:	SNACKS:	SNACKS:

NOTES:

Expenses

Agenda

To do list

MONDAY	TUESDAY	WEDNESDAY
BREAKFAST:	BREAKFAST:	BREAKFAST:
LUNCH:	LUNCH:	LUNCH:
DINNER:	DINNER:	DINNER:
SNACKS:	SNACKS:	SNACKS:

THURSDAY	FRIDAY	SATURDAY	SUNDAY
BREAKFAST:	BREAKFAST:	BREAKFAST:	BREAKFAST:
LUNCH:	LUNCH:	LUNCH:	LUNCH:
DINNER:	DINNER:	DINNER:	DINNER:
SNACKS:	SNACKS:	SNACKS:	SNACKS:

NOTES:

Expenses

Agenda

To do list

MONDAY	TUESDAY	WEDNESDAY
BREAKFAST:	BREAKFAST:	BREAKFAST:
LUNCH:	LUNCH:	LUNCH:
DINNER:	DINNER:	DINNER:
SNACKS:	SNACKS:	SNACKS:

THURSDAY	FRIDAY	SATURDAY	SUNDAY
BREAKFAST:	BREAKFAST:	BREAKFAST:	BREAKFAST:
LUNCH:	LUNCH:	LUNCH:	LUNCH:
DINNER:	DINNER:	DINNER:	DINNER:
SNACKS:	SNACKS:	SNACKS:	SNACKS:

NOTES:

Expenses

Agenda

To do list

MONDAY	TUESDAY	WEDNESDAY
BREAKFAST:	BREAKFAST:	BREAKFAST:
LUNCH:	LUNCH:	LUNCH:
DINNER:	DINNER:	DINNER:
SNACKS:	SNACKS:	SNACKS:

THURSDAY	FRIDAY	SATURDAY	SUNDAY
BREAKFAST:	BREAKFAST:	BREAKFAST:	BREAKFAST:
LUNCH:	LUNCH:	LUNCH:	LUNCH:
DINNER:	DINNER:	DINNER:	DINNER:
SNACKS:	SNACKS:	SNACKS:	SNACKS:

NOTES:

Expenses

Agenda

To do list

MONDAY	TUESDAY	WEDNESDAY
BREAKFAST:	**BREAKFAST:**	**BREAKFAST:**
LUNCH:	LUNCH:	LUNCH:
DINNER:	DINNER:	DINNER:
SNACKS:	**SNACKS:**	**SNACKS:**

THURSDAY	FRIDAY	SATURDAY	SUNDAY
BREAKFAST:	BREAKFAST:	BREAKFAST:	BREAKFAST:
LUNCH:	LUNCH:	LUNCH:	LUNCH:
DINNER:	DINNER:	DINNER:	DINNER:
SNACKS:	SNACKS:	SNACKS:	SNACKS:

NOTES:

Expenses

Agenda

To do list

MONDAY	TUESDAY	WEDNESDAY
BREAKFAST:	BREAKFAST:	BREAKFAST:
LUNCH:	LUNCH:	LUNCH:
DINNER:	DINNER:	DINNER:
SNACKS:	SNACKS:	SNACKS:

THURSDAY	FRIDAY	SATURDAY	SUNDAY
BREAKFAST:	BREAKFAST:	BREAKFAST:	BREAKFAST:
LUNCH:	LUNCH:	LUNCH:	LUNCH:
DINNER:	DINNER:	DINNER:	DINNER:
SNACKS:	SNACKS:	SNACKS:	SNACKS:

NOTES:

Expenses

Agenda

To do list

MONDAY	TUESDAY	WEDNESDAY
BREAKFAST:	BREAKFAST:	BREAKFAST:
LUNCH:	LUNCH:	LUNCH:
DINNER:	DINNER:	DINNER:
SNACKS:	SNACKS:	SNACKS:

THURSDAY	FRIDAY	SATURDAY	SUNDAY
BREAKFAST:	BREAKFAST:	BREAKFAST:	BREAKFAST:
LUNCH:	LUNCH:	LUNCH:	LUNCH:
DINNER:	DINNER:	DINNER:	DINNER:
SNACKS:	SNACKS:	SNACKS:	SNACKS:

NOTES:

_____
_____
_____
_____
_____
_____
_____
_____
_____
_____
_____
_____
_____
_____
_____
_____
_____
_____
_____
_____
_____
_____

Expenses

Agenda

To do list

MONDAY	TUESDAY	WEDNESDAY
BREAKFAST:	BREAKFAST:	BREAKFAST:
LUNCH:	LUNCH:	LUNCH:
DINNER:	DINNER:	DINNER:
SNACKS:	SNACKS:	SNACKS:

THURSDAY	FRIDAY	SATURDAY	SUNDAY
BREAKFAST:	BREAKFAST:	BREAKFAST:	BREAKFAST:
LUNCH:	LUNCH:	LUNCH:	LUNCH:
DINNER:	DINNER:	DINNER:	DINNER:
SNACKS:	SNACKS:	SNACKS:	SNACKS:

NOTES:

Expenses

Agenda

To do list

MONDAY	TUESDAY	WEDNESDAY
BREAKFAST:	**BREAKFAST:**	**BREAKFAST:**
LUNCH:	**LUNCH:**	**LUNCH:**
DINNER:	**DINNER:**	**DINNER:**
SNACKS:	**SNACKS:**	**SNACKS:**

THURSDAY	FRIDAY	SATURDAY	SUNDAY
BREAKFAST:	BREAKFAST:	BREAKFAST:	BREAKFAST:
LUNCH:	LUNCH:	LUNCH:	LUNCH:
DINNER:	DINNER:	DINNER:	DINNER:
SNACKS:	SNACKS:	SNACKS:	SNACKS:

NOTES:

Expenses

Agenda

To do list

MONDAY	TUESDAY	WEDNESDAY
BREAKFAST:	BREAKFAST:	BREAKFAST:
LUNCH:	LUNCH:	LUNCH:
DINNER:	DINNER:	DINNER:
SNACKS:	SNACKS:	SNACKS:

THURSDAY	FRIDAY	SATURDAY	SUNDAY
BREAKFAST:	BREAKFAST:	BREAKFAST:	BREAKFAST:
LUNCH:	LUNCH:	LUNCH:	LUNCH:
DINNER:	DINNER:	DINNER:	DINNER:
SNACKS:	SNACKS:	SNACKS:	SNACKS:

NOTES:

Expenses

Agenda

To do list

MONDAY	TUESDAY	WEDNESDAY
BREAKFAST:	BREAKFAST:	BREAKFAST:
LUNCH:	LUNCH:	LUNCH:
DINNER:	DINNER:	DINNER:
SNACKS:	SNACKS:	SNACKS:

THURSDAY	FRIDAY	SATURDAY	SUNDAY
BREAKFAST:	BREAKFAST:	BREAKFAST:	BREAKFAST:
LUNCH:	LUNCH:	LUNCH:	LUNCH:
DINNER:	DINNER:	DINNER:	DINNER:
SNACKS:	SNACKS:	SNACKS:	SNACKS:

NOTES:

_____
_____
_____
_____
_____
_____
_____
_____
_____
_____
_____
_____
_____
_____
_____
_____
_____
_____
_____
_____
_____
_____
_____

Expenses

Agenda

To do list

MONDAY	TUESDAY	WEDNESDAY
BREAKFAST:	BREAKFAST:	BREAKFAST:
LUNCH:	LUNCH:	LUNCH:
DINNER:	DINNER:	DINNER:
SNACKS:	SNACKS:	SNACKS:

THURSDAY	FRIDAY	SATURDAY	SUNDAY
BREAKFAST:	BREAKFAST:	BREAKFAST:	BREAKFAST:
LUNCH:	LUNCH:	LUNCH:	LUNCH:
DINNER:	DINNER:	DINNER:	DINNER:
SNACKS:	SNACKS:	SNACKS:	SNACKS:

NOTES:

_____

_____

_____

_____

_____

_____

_____

_____

_____

_____

_____

_____

_____

_____

_____

_____

_____

_____

_____

_____

_____

_____

_____

_____

Expenses

Agenda

To do list

MONDAY	TUESDAY	WEDNESDAY
BREAKFAST:	BREAKFAST:	BREAKFAST:
LUNCH:	LUNCH:	LUNCH:
DINNER:	DINNER:	DINNER:
SNACKS:	SNACKS:	SNACKS:

THURSDAY	FRIDAY	SATURDAY	SUNDAY
BREAKFAST:	BREAKFAST:	BREAKFAST:	BREAKFAST:
LUNCH:	LUNCH:	LUNCH:	LUNCH:
DINNER:	DINNER:	DINNER:	DINNER:
SNACKS:	SNACKS:	SNACKS:	SNACKS:

NOTES:

_____
_____
_____
_____
_____
_____
_____
_____
_____
_____
_____
_____
_____
_____
_____
_____
_____
_____
_____
_____
_____
_____
_____
_____

Expenses

Agenda

To do list

MONDAY	TUESDAY	WEDNESDAY
BREAKFAST:	BREAKFAST:	BREAKFAST:
LUNCH:	LUNCH:	LUNCH:
DINNER:	DINNER:	DINNER:
SNACKS:	SNACKS:	SNACKS:

THURSDAY	FRIDAY	SATURDAY	SUNDAY
BREAKFAST:	BREAKFAST:	BREAKFAST:	BREAKFAST:
LUNCH:	LUNCH:	LUNCH:	LUNCH:
DINNER:	DINNER:	DINNER:	DINNER:
SNACKS:	SNACKS:	SNACKS:	SNACKS:

NOTES:

Expenses

Agenda

To do list

MONDAY	TUESDAY	WEDNESDAY
BREAKFAST:	**BREAKFAST:**	**BREAKFAST:**
LUNCH:	**LUNCH:**	**LUNCH:**
DINNER:	**DINNER:**	**DINNER:**
SNACKS:	**SNACKS:**	**SNACKS:**

THURSDAY	FRIDAY	SATURDAY	SUNDAY
BREAKFAST:	BREAKFAST:	BREAKFAST:	BREAKFAST:
LUNCH:	LUNCH:	LUNCH:	LUNCH:
DINNER:	DINNER:	DINNER:	DINNER:
SNACKS:	SNACKS:	SNACKS:	SNACKS:

NOTES:

Expenses

Agenda

To do list

MONDAY	TUESDAY	WEDNESDAY
BREAKFAST:	BREAKFAST:	BREAKFAST:
LUNCH:	LUNCH:	LUNCH:
DINNER:	DINNER:	DINNER:
SNACKS:	SNACKS:	SNACKS:

THURSDAY	FRIDAY	SATURDAY	SUNDAY
BREAKFAST:	BREAKFAST:	BREAKFAST:	BREAKFAST:
LUNCH:	LUNCH:	LUNCH:	LUNCH:
DINNER:	DINNER:	DINNER:	DINNER:
SNACKS:	SNACKS:	SNACKS:	SNACKS:

NOTES:

Expenses

Agenda

To do list

MONDAY	TUESDAY	WEDNESDAY
BREAKFAST:	BREAKFAST:	BREAKFAST:
LUNCH:	LUNCH:	LUNCH:
DINNER:	DINNER:	DINNER:
SNACKS:	SNACKS:	SNACKS:

THURSDAY	FRIDAY	SATURDAY	SUNDAY
BREAKFAST:	BREAKFAST:	BREAKFAST:	BREAKFAST:
LUNCH:	LUNCH:	LUNCH:	LUNCH:
DINNER:	DINNER:	DINNER:	DINNER:
SNACKS:	SNACKS:	SNACKS:	SNACKS:

NOTES:

Expenses

Agenda

To do list

MONDAY	TUESDAY	WEDNESDAY
BREAKFAST:	BREAKFAST:	BREAKFAST:
LUNCH:	LUNCH:	LUNCH:
DINNER:	DINNER:	DINNER:
SNACKS:	SNACKS:	SNACKS:

THURSDAY	FRIDAY	SATURDAY	SUNDAY
BREAKFAST:	BREAKFAST:	BREAKFAST:	BREAKFAST:
LUNCH:	LUNCH:	LUNCH:	LUNCH:
DINNER:	DINNER:	DINNER:	DINNER:
SNACKS:	SNACKS:	SNACKS:	SNACKS:

NOTES:

Expenses

Agenda

To do list

MONDAY	TUESDAY	WEDNESDAY
BREAKFAST:	BREAKFAST:	BREAKFAST:
LUNCH:	LUNCH:	LUNCH:
DINNER:	DINNER:	DINNER:
SNACKS:	SNACKS:	SNACKS:

THURSDAY	FRIDAY	SATURDAY	SUNDAY
BREAKFAST:	BREAKFAST:	BREAKFAST:	BREAKFAST:
LUNCH:	LUNCH:	LUNCH:	LUNCH:
DINNER:	DINNER:	DINNER:	DINNER:
SNACKS:	SNACKS:	SNACKS:	SNACKS:

NOTES:

Expenses

Agenda

To do list

MONDAY	TUESDAY	WEDNESDAY
BREAKFAST:	BREAKFAST:	BREAKFAST:
LUNCH:	LUNCH:	LUNCH:
DINNER:	DINNER:	DINNER:
SNACKS:	SNACKS:	SNACKS:

THURSDAY	FRIDAY	SATURDAY	SUNDAY
BREAKFAST:	BREAKFAST:	BREAKFAST:	BREAKFAST:
LUNCH:	LUNCH:	LUNCH:	LUNCH:
DINNER:	DINNER:	DINNER:	DINNER:
SNACKS:	SNACKS:	SNACKS:	SNACKS:

NOTES:

Expenses

Agenda

To do list

MONDAY	TUESDAY	WEDNESDAY
BREAKFAST:	BREAKFAST:	BREAKFAST:
LUNCH:	LUNCH:	LUNCH:
DINNER:	DINNER:	DINNER:
SNACKS:	SNACKS:	SNACKS:

THURSDAY	FRIDAY	SATURDAY	SUNDAY
BREAKFAST:	BREAKFAST:	BREAKFAST:	BREAKFAST:
LUNCH:	LUNCH:	LUNCH:	LUNCH:
DINNER:	DINNER:	DINNER:	DINNER:
SNACKS:	SNACKS:	SNACKS:	SNACKS:

NOTES:

Expenses

Agenda

To do list

MONDAY	TUESDAY	WEDNESDAY
BREAKFAST:	BREAKFAST:	BREAKFAST:
LUNCH:	LUNCH:	LUNCH:
DINNER:	DINNER:	DINNER:
SNACKS:	SNACKS:	SNACKS:

THURSDAY	FRIDAY	SATURDAY	SUNDAY
BREAKFAST:	BREAKFAST:	BREAKFAST:	BREAKFAST:
LUNCH:	LUNCH:	LUNCH:	LUNCH:
DINNER:	DINNER:	DINNER:	DINNER:
SNACKS:	SNACKS:	SNACKS:	SNACKS:

NOTES:

Expenses

Agenda

To do list

MONDAY	TUESDAY	WEDNESDAY
BREAKFAST:	BREAKFAST:	BREAKFAST:
LUNCH:	LUNCH:	LUNCH:
DINNER:	DINNER:	DINNER:
SNACKS:	SNACKS:	SNACKS:

THURSDAY	FRIDAY	SATURDAY	SUNDAY
BREAKFAST:	BREAKFAST:	BREAKFAST:	BREAKFAST:
LUNCH:	LUNCH:	LUNCH:	LUNCH:
DINNER:	DINNER:	DINNER:	DINNER:
SNACKS:	SNACKS:	SNACKS:	SNACKS:

NOTES:

Expenses

Agenda

To do list

MONDAY	TUESDAY	WEDNESDAY
BREAKFAST:	BREAKFAST:	BREAKFAST:
LUNCH:	LUNCH:	LUNCH:
DINNER:	DINNER:	DINNER:
SNACKS:	SNACKS:	SNACKS:

THURSDAY	FRIDAY	SATURDAY	SUNDAY
BREAKFAST:	BREAKFAST:	BREAKFAST:	BREAKFAST:
LUNCH:	LUNCH:	LUNCH:	LUNCH:
DINNER:	DINNER:	DINNER:	DINNER:
SNACKS:	SNACKS:	SNACKS:	SNACKS:

NOTES:

Expenses

Agenda

To do list

MONDAY	TUESDAY	WEDNESDAY
BREAKFAST:	BREAKFAST:	BREAKFAST:
LUNCH:	LUNCH:	LUNCH:
DINNER:	DINNER:	DINNER:
SNACKS:	SNACKS:	SNACKS:

THURSDAY	FRIDAY	SATURDAY	SUNDAY
BREAKFAST:	BREAKFAST:	BREAKFAST:	BREAKFAST:
LUNCH:	LUNCH:	LUNCH:	LUNCH:
DINNER:	DINNER:	DINNER:	DINNER:
SNACKS:	SNACKS:	SNACKS:	SNACKS:

NOTES:

Expenses

Agenda

To do list

MONDAY	TUESDAY	WEDNESDAY
BREAKFAST:	BREAKFAST:	BREAKFAST:
LUNCH:	LUNCH:	LUNCH:
DINNER:	DINNER:	DINNER:
SNACKS:	SNACKS:	SNACKS:

THURSDAY	FRIDAY	SATURDAY	SUNDAY
BREAKFAST:	BREAKFAST:	BREAKFAST:	BREAKFAST:
LUNCH:	LUNCH:	LUNCH:	LUNCH:
DINNER:	DINNER:	DINNER:	DINNER:
SNACKS:	SNACKS:	SNACKS:	SNACKS:

NOTES:

Expenses

Agenda

To do list

MONDAY	TUESDAY	WEDNESDAY
BREAKFAST:	BREAKFAST:	BREAKFAST:
LUNCH:	LUNCH:	LUNCH:
DINNER:	DINNER:	DINNER:
SNACKS:	SNACKS:	SNACKS:

THURSDAY	FRIDAY	SATURDAY	SUNDAY
BREAKFAST:	BREAKFAST:	BREAKFAST:	BREAKFAST:
LUNCH:	LUNCH:	LUNCH:	LUNCH:
DINNER:	DINNER:	DINNER:	DINNER:
SNACKS:	SNACKS:	SNACKS:	SNACKS:

NOTES:

Expenses

Agenda

To do list

MONDAY	TUESDAY	WEDNESDAY
BREAKFAST:	BREAKFAST:	BREAKFAST:
LUNCH:	LUNCH:	LUNCH:
DINNER:	DINNER:	DINNER:
SNACKS:	SNACKS:	SNACKS:

THURSDAY	FRIDAY	SATURDAY	SUNDAY
BREAKFAST:	BREAKFAST:	BREAKFAST:	BREAKFAST:
LUNCH:	LUNCH:	LUNCH:	LUNCH:
DINNER:	DINNER:	DINNER:	DINNER:
SNACKS:	SNACKS:	SNACKS:	SNACKS:

NOTES:

Expenses

Agenda

To do list

MONDAY	TUESDAY	WEDNESDAY
BREAKFAST:	BREAKFAST:	BREAKFAST:
LUNCH:	LUNCH:	LUNCH:
DINNER:	DINNER:	DINNER:
SNACKS:	SNACKS:	SNACKS:

THURSDAY	FRIDAY	SATURDAY	SUNDAY
BREAKFAST:	BREAKFAST:	BREAKFAST:	BREAKFAST:
LUNCH:	LUNCH:	LUNCH:	LUNCH:
DINNER:	DINNER:	DINNER:	DINNER:
SNACKS:	SNACKS:	SNACKS:	SNACKS:

NOTES:

Expenses

Agenda

To do list

MONDAY	TUESDAY	WEDNESDAY
BREAKFAST:	BREAKFAST:	BREAKFAST:
LUNCH:	LUNCH:	LUNCH:
DINNER:	DINNER:	DINNER:
SNACKS:	SNACKS:	SNACKS:

THURSDAY	FRIDAY	SATURDAY	SUNDAY
BREAKFAST:	BREAKFAST:	BREAKFAST:	BREAKFAST:
LUNCH:	LUNCH:	LUNCH:	LUNCH:
DINNER:	DINNER:	DINNER:	DINNER:
SNACKS:	SNACKS:	SNACKS:	SNACKS:

NOTES:

Expenses

Agenda

To do list

MONDAY	TUESDAY	WEDNESDAY
BREAKFAST:	BREAKFAST:	BREAKFAST:
LUNCH:	LUNCH:	LUNCH:
DINNER:	DINNER:	DINNER:
SNACKS:	SNACKS:	SNACKS:

THURSDAY	FRIDAY	SATURDAY	SUNDAY
BREAKFAST:	BREAKFAST:	BREAKFAST:	BREAKFAST:
LUNCH:	LUNCH:	LUNCH:	LUNCH:
DINNER:	DINNER:	DINNER:	DINNER:
SNACKS:	SNACKS:	SNACKS:	SNACKS:

NOTES:

Expenses

Agenda

To do list

MONDAY	TUESDAY	WEDNESDAY
BREAKFAST:	BREAKFAST:	BREAKFAST:
LUNCH:	LUNCH:	LUNCH:
DINNER:	DINNER:	DINNER:
SNACKS:	SNACKS:	SNACKS:

THURSDAY	FRIDAY	SATURDAY	SUNDAY
BREAKFAST:	BREAKFAST:	BREAKFAST:	BREAKFAST:
LUNCH:	LUNCH:	LUNCH:	LUNCH:
DINNER:	DINNER:	DINNER:	DINNER:
SNACKS:	SNACKS:	SNACKS:	SNACKS:

NOTES:

Expenses

Agenda

To do list

MONDAY	TUESDAY	WEDNESDAY
BREAKFAST:	BREAKFAST:	BREAKFAST:
LUNCH:	LUNCH:	LUNCH:
DINNER:	DINNER:	DINNER:
SNACKS:	SNACKS:	SNACKS:

THURSDAY	FRIDAY	SATURDAY	SUNDAY
BREAKFAST:	BREAKFAST:	BREAKFAST:	BREAKFAST:
LUNCH:	LUNCH:	LUNCH:	LUNCH:
DINNER:	DINNER:	DINNER:	DINNER:
SNACKS:	SNACKS:	SNACKS:	SNACKS:

NOTES:

_____
_____
_____
_____
_____
_____
_____
_____
_____
_____
_____
_____
_____
_____
_____
_____
_____
_____
_____
_____
_____

Expenses

Agenda

To do list

MONDAY	TUESDAY	WEDNESDAY
BREAKFAST:	BREAKFAST:	BREAKFAST:
LUNCH:	LUNCH:	LUNCH:
DINNER:	DINNER:	DINNER:
SNACKS:	SNACKS:	SNACKS:

THURSDAY	FRIDAY	SATURDAY	SUNDAY
BREAKFAST:	BREAKFAST:	BREAKFAST:	BREAKFAST:
LUNCH:	LUNCH:	LUNCH:	LUNCH:
DINNER:	DINNER:	DINNER:	DINNER:
SNACKS:	SNACKS:	SNACKS:	SNACKS:

NOTES:

Expenses

Agenda

To do list

MONDAY	TUESDAY	WEDNESDAY
BREAKFAST:	BREAKFAST:	BREAKFAST:
LUNCH:	LUNCH:	LUNCH:
DINNER:	DINNER:	DINNER:
SNACKS:	SNACKS:	SNACKS:

THURSDAY	FRIDAY	SATURDAY	SUNDAY
BREAKFAST:	BREAKFAST:	BREAKFAST:	BREAKFAST:
LUNCH:	LUNCH:	LUNCH:	LUNCH:
DINNER:	DINNER:	DINNER:	DINNER:
SNACKS:	SNACKS:	SNACKS:	SNACKS:

NOTES:

Expenses

Agenda

To do list

MONDAY	TUESDAY	WEDNESDAY
BREAKFAST:	BREAKFAST:	BREAKFAST:
LUNCH:	LUNCH:	LUNCH:
DINNER:	DINNER:	DINNER:
SNACKS:	SNACKS:	SNACKS:

THURSDAY	FRIDAY	SATURDAY	SUNDAY
BREAKFAST:	BREAKFAST:	BREAKFAST:	BREAKFAST:
LUNCH:	LUNCH:	LUNCH:	LUNCH:
DINNER:	DINNER:	DINNER:	DINNER:
SNACKS:	SNACKS:	SNACKS:	SNACKS:

NOTES:

Expenses

Agenda

To do list

MONDAY	TUESDAY	WEDNESDAY
BREAKFAST:	BREAKFAST:	BREAKFAST:
LUNCH:	LUNCH:	LUNCH:
DINNER:	DINNER:	DINNER:
SNACKS:	SNACKS:	SNACKS:

THURSDAY	FRIDAY	SATURDAY	SUNDAY
BREAKFAST:	BREAKFAST:	BREAKFAST:	BREAKFAST:
LUNCH:	LUNCH:	LUNCH:	LUNCH:
DINNER:	DINNER:	DINNER:	DINNER:
SNACKS:	SNACKS:	SNACKS:	SNACKS:

NOTES:

Expenses

Agenda

To do list

MONDAY	TUESDAY	WEDNESDAY
BREAKFAST:	BREAKFAST:	BREAKFAST:
LUNCH:	LUNCH:	LUNCH:
DINNER:	DINNER:	DINNER:
SNACKS:	SNACKS:	SNACKS:

THURSDAY	FRIDAY	SATURDAY	SUNDAY
BREAKFAST:	BREAKFAST:	BREAKFAST:	BREAKFAST:
LUNCH:	LUNCH:	LUNCH:	LUNCH:
DINNER:	DINNER:	DINNER:	DINNER:
SNACKS:	SNACKS:	SNACKS:	SNACKS:

NOTES:

Expenses

Agenda

To do list

MONDAY	TUESDAY	WEDNESDAY
BREAKFAST:	BREAKFAST:	BREAKFAST:
LUNCH:	LUNCH:	LUNCH:
DINNER:	DINNER:	DINNER:
SNACKS:	SNACKS:	SNACKS:

THURSDAY	FRIDAY	SATURDAY	SUNDAY
BREAKFAST:	BREAKFAST:	BREAKFAST:	BREAKFAST:
LUNCH:	LUNCH:	LUNCH:	LUNCH:
DINNER:	DINNER:	DINNER:	DINNER:
SNACKS:	SNACKS:	SNACKS:	SNACKS:

NOTES:

Expenses

Agenda

To do list

MONDAY	TUESDAY	WEDNESDAY
BREAKFAST:	BREAKFAST:	BREAKFAST:
LUNCH:	LUNCH:	LUNCH:
DINNER:	DINNER:	DINNER:
SNACKS:	SNACKS:	SNACKS:

THURSDAY	FRIDAY	SATURDAY	SUNDAY
BREAKFAST:	BREAKFAST:	BREAKFAST:	BREAKFAST:
LUNCH:	LUNCH:	LUNCH:	LUNCH:
DINNER:	DINNER:	DINNER:	DINNER:
SNACKS:	SNACKS:	SNACKS:	SNACKS:

NOTES:

Expenses

Agenda

To do list

MONDAY	TUESDAY	WEDNESDAY
BREAKFAST:	BREAKFAST:	BREAKFAST:
LUNCH:	LUNCH:	LUNCH:
DINNER:	DINNER:	DINNER:
SNACKS:	SNACKS:	SNACKS:

THURSDAY	FRIDAY	SATURDAY	SUNDAY
BREAKFAST:	BREAKFAST:	BREAKFAST:	BREAKFAST:
LUNCH:	LUNCH:	LUNCH:	LUNCH:
DINNER:	DINNER:	DINNER:	DINNER:
SNACKS:	SNACKS:	SNACKS:	SNACKS:

NOTES:

Expenses

Agenda

To do list

MONDAY	TUESDAY	WEDNESDAY
BREAKFAST:	**BREAKFAST:**	**BREAKFAST:**
LUNCH:	**LUNCH:**	**LUNCH:**
DINNER:	**DINNER:**	**DINNER:**
SNACKS:	**SNACKS:**	**SNACKS:**

THURSDAY	FRIDAY	SATURDAY	SUNDAY
BREAKFAST:	BREAKFAST:	BREAKFAST:	BREAKFAST:
LUNCH:	LUNCH:	LUNCH:	LUNCH:
DINNER:	DINNER:	DINNER:	DINNER:
SNACKS:	SNACKS:	SNACKS:	SNACKS:

NOTES:

www.ingramcontent.com/pod-product-compliance
Lightning Source LLC
Chambersburg PA
CBHW080737250626
47170CB00010B/2860